Spotlight on India

Robin Johnson & Bobbie Kalman

Crabtree Publishing
crabtreebooks.com

Spotlight On My Country

Created by Bobbie Kalman

Dedicated b yRobin Johnson
For Dean, a great soul

Crabtree Publishing

crabtreebooks.com 800-387-7650

Editor-in-Chief: Bobbie Kalman
Writing team: Robin Johnson, Bobbie Kalman
Edltor: Michael Hodge
Photo research: Bobbie Kalman, Robin Johnson, Crystal Sikkens
Design: Katherine Kantor, Samantha Crabtree (cover)
Production manager: Candice Campbell

Hardcover 978-0-7787-3455-0
Paperback 978-0-7787-3481-9

Printed in the U.S.A./CP062026

Library and Archives Canada Cataloguing in Publication
Johnson, Robin (Robin R.)
Spotlight on India / Robin Johnson & Bobbie Kalman.

(Spotlight on my country)
Includes index.
ISBN 978-0-7787-3455-0 (bound).--
ISBN 978-0-7787-3481-9 (pbk.)

1. India--Juvenile literature. I. Kalman, Bobbie, 1947- II. Title. III. Series.

DS407.J64 2008 j954 C2008-901028-0

Published in Canada
Crabtree Publishing
616 Welland Avenue
St. Catharines, Ontario
L2M 5V6

Published in the United States
Crabtree Publishing
347 Fifth Avenue
Suite 1402-145
New York, NY 10016

Illustrations:
William Band: pages 16, 17
Barbara Bedell: page 13 (cotton)
Katherine Kantor: pages 4, 5
Robert MacGregor: page 13 (rice)
Renée Mansfield: pages 20-21
John Mantha: page 13 (wheat)
Diane Rome Peebles: page 13 (fish)
Bonna Rouse: page 23

Photographs:
© Dreamstime.com: back cover (masks), pages 4, 9 (bottom), 13 (top), 14, 15 (top left), 21, 25 (bottom), 30 (top and bottom left), 31 (masks)
© iStockphoto.com: pages 3, 10 (bottom right), 22, 23 (top), 28 (naan), 29 (bottom right)
© 2008 Jupiterimages Corporation: pages 18 (bottom), 19, 24 (top), 26 (bottom left)
© Shutterstock.com: cover (except masks), pages 1, 5, 6, 7 (bottom), 8, 9 (top), 10 (top and bottom left), 11, 12, 13 (bottom), 15 (top right and bottom left), 18 (top), 23 (bottom), 24 (bottom), 25 (top and middle), 26 (top and bottom, right), 27, 28 (except naan), 29 (top and bottom left), 30 (bottom right), 31 (except masks)
Other images by Corel

Library of Congress Cataloging-in-Publication Data
Johnson, Robin (Robin R.)
Spotlight on India / Robin Johnson and Bobbie Kalman.
p. cm. -- (Spotlight on my country)
Includes index.
ISBN-13: 978-0-7787-3455-0 (rlb)
ISBN-10: 0-7787-3455-2 (rlb)
ISBN-13: 978-0-7787-3481-9 (pbk.)
ISBN-10: 0-7787-3481-1 (pbk.)
1. India--Juvenile literature. I. Kalman, Bobbie. II. Title.
DS407.J65 2008
954--dc22

2008005108

Contents

Welcome to India!

Welcome to India! India is a large **country**. A country has people. Its people must follow **laws**, or rules. A country also has **borders**. Borders separate areas of land into countries. India shares its borders with six other countries. Find India and its neighbors on this map.

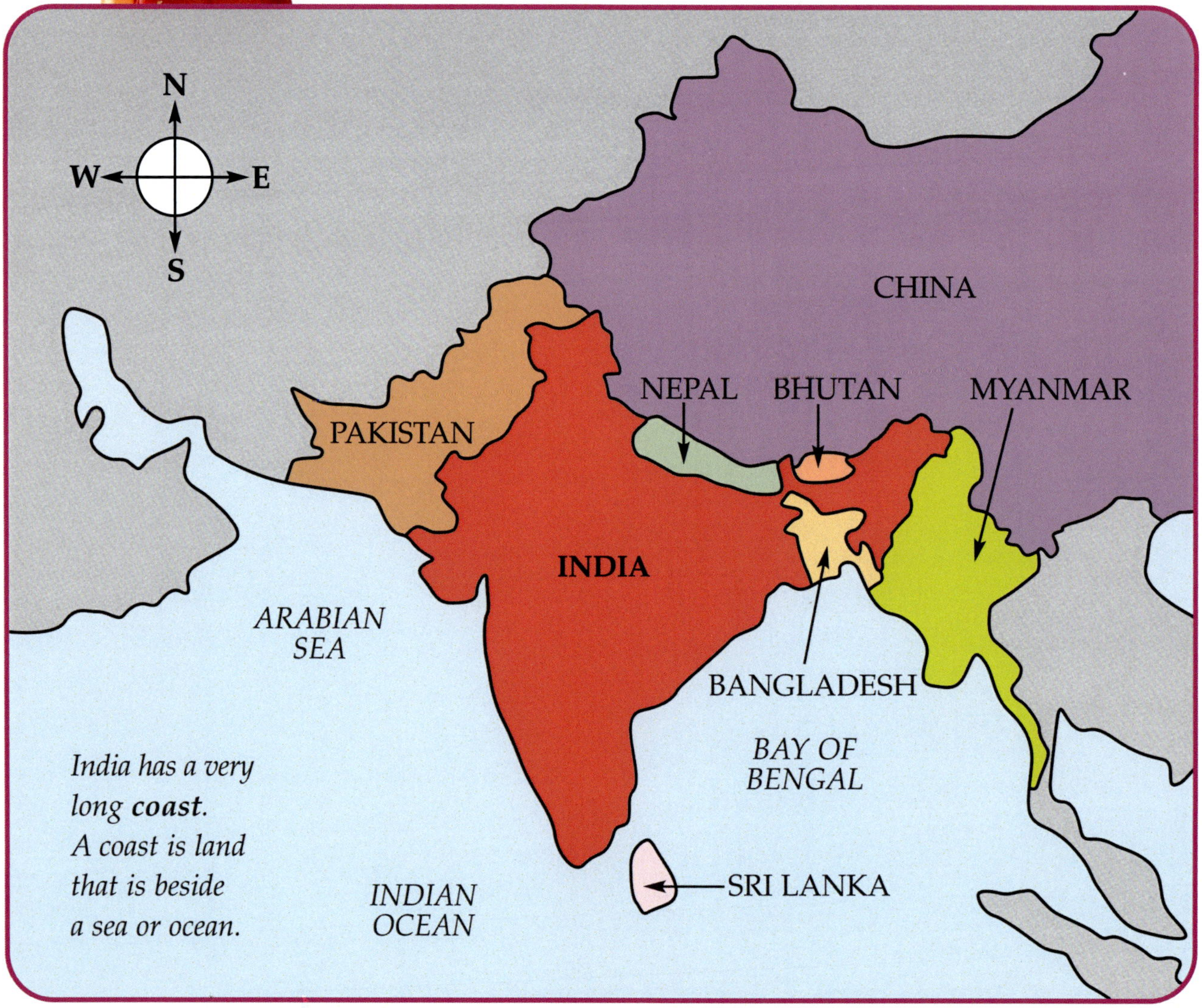

India has a very long ***coast****. A coast is land that is beside a sea or ocean.*

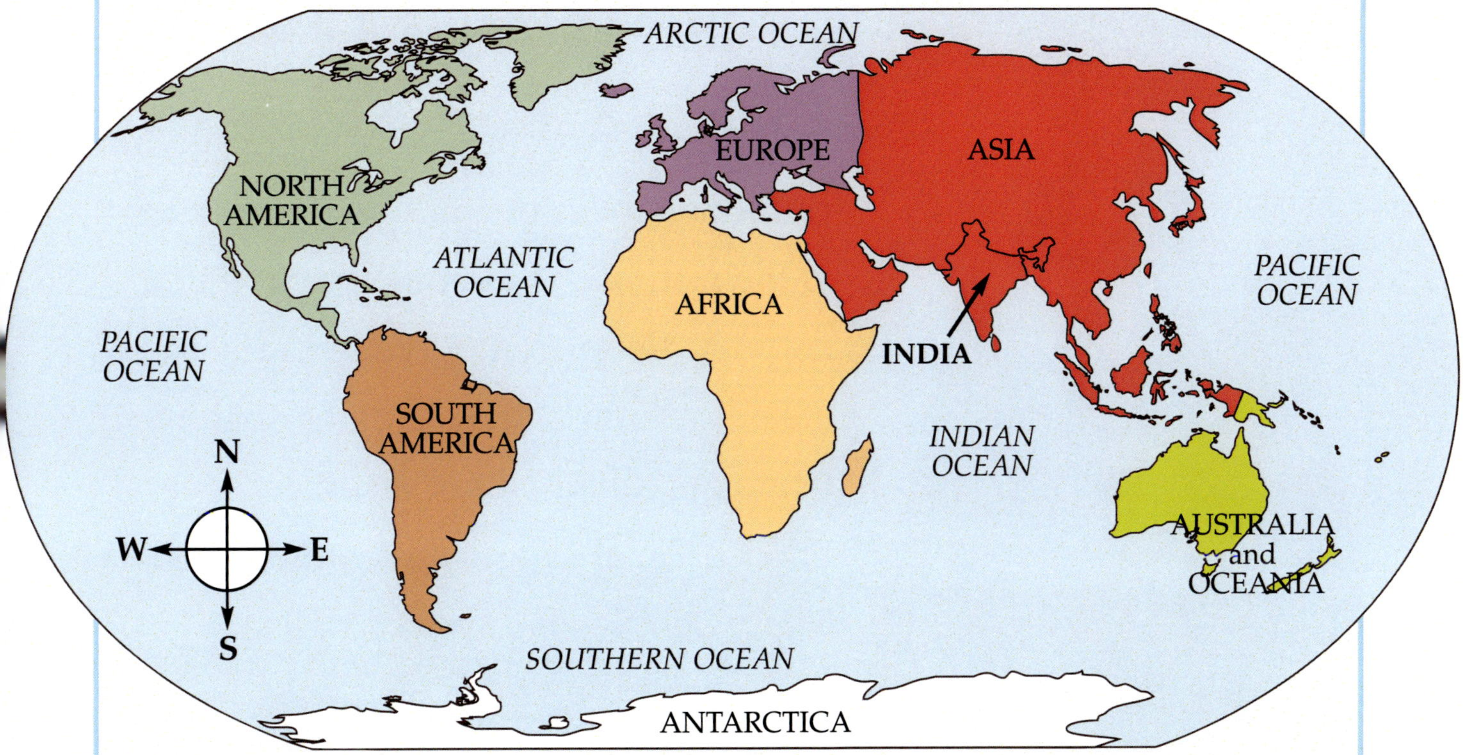

Where on Earth is India?

India is part of the **continent** of Asia. A continent is a huge area of land. There are seven continents on Earth. They are Asia, North America, South America, Europe, Africa, Australia and Oceania, and Antarctica. Asia is the largest continent in the world. Find Asia and India on the map above.

The people of India

India has a lot of people! The **population** of India is over one billion. Population is the number of people who live in a country. People who live in India are called Indians. Many Indians speak a language called Hindi. There are several other **official languages** in India, too. Many people also speak English.

Different lives

The people of India lead different ways of life. Their languages, beliefs, customs, and **religions** are not all the same. Even though people may be different from one another, they live together peacefully in their country.

The children on this boat are waving Indian flags. The sign says "We are one." What do you think it means?

Family is very important in India. In many homes, children, parents, aunts, uncles, cousins, and grandparents all live together. How many people are part of this family?

India's land

There are huge deserts in India. Few plants grow in these hot, dry lands. Camels are animals that can live in deserts.

There are many **landscapes** in India. A landscape is how land looks. India has dry **deserts**, green **valleys**, high mountains, and flat **plains**. Some of India's landscapes are shown on these pages.

There are beautiful green valleys in India. A valley is low land that is between hills or mountains.

*There are many mountains in India. Some huge mountains are covered with snow all year. Other smaller mountains have mild **climates**. Climate is the usual weather in an area.*

*Many Indians live on plains. Plains are flat lands with a few trees. India's large plains are good for growing **crops**. Crops are plants that people grow for food and other uses.*

Wild weather

India's land is often damaged by severe weather. **Floods** or **droughts** destroy crops. **Earthquakes** shake the ground and damage the land. In 2004, a **tsunami** hit the coast of India. A tsunami is one or more huge, tall waves. The tsunami killed thousands of people and destroyed many homes.

This city bridge is covered by flood water.

Plants and animals

There are many kinds of plants and animals in India. They grow or live in different parts of the country. Each kind of plant or animal is suited to the place where it lives.

*The lotus is India's **national** flower. National means belonging to a country. Lotuses grow in ponds.*

Red pandas live in forests on India's mountains. The pandas eat the bamboo plants that grow in the forests.

*Camels live in India's dry deserts. They can survive for several days without water. This baby camel is **nursing**, or drinking milk from its mother's body.*

Holy cows

Most people in India believe cows to be **sacred**, or holy. Cows are respected for their gentle ways and for the milk they give. People drink the milk and use it to make butter and cheese. In many parts of India, it is against the law to kill cows or harm them in any way.

Royal Bengal tigers live on plains and in forests. They are ***endangered*** *animals. Endangered animals are in danger of dying out in the wild.*

Asian elephants are working animals in India. They are trained to pull up trees and move heavy logs in Indian forests. People also ride these animals.

*Many Indian villages have no running water. People get water from **wells**, rivers, or lakes. This girl is filling her water jug at a lake, which is **polluted**, or very dirty.*

Village life

Most Indians live in **villages**. A village is a small town in the countryside. In most Indian villages, there is a **bazaar**, or outdoor market, and a village **square**. A square is an area where people meet. The homes in a village are usually built around the village square.

These children and their families live and work in a small village in the countryside.

Farming and fishing

Many Indians are farmers. They grow crops in fields near their villages. Farmers in India grow rice, wheat, sugar cane, peanuts, bananas, tea, cotton, and many other crops. Other Indians fish for food. They live in fishing villages on the coast.

Much farm work is done by hand. These children are picking tomatoes. Many children in India must work to help their families.

fish

wheat

cotton

rice

These Indian fishermen are using large nets to catch fish on the coast.

India's busy cities

*These **rickshas** are speeding through a city street. A ricksha is a small three-wheeled car that can carry a driver and one or two passengers.*

Many Indians live in big cities. India's cities are busy, noisy places! They are crowded with people, shops, street **vendors**, theaters, and factories. One of the biggest cities in India is New Delhi. It is the **capital** of the country.

The streets of New Delhi are crowded with people, cars, bicycles, and rickshas.

Mumbai is a big business center. It is the most crowded city in the world! Mumbai used to be called Bombay.

There are not enough jobs or homes for everyone in India's crowded cities. Many people must live on the streets.

Varanasi, also known as Benares, is on the Ganges River. People call Varanasi the "city of ***temples****" and the "holy city." People of all religions visit this city.*

Some Indians are wealthy. They live in large, comfortable homes. This family is celebrating a wedding. Everyone is dressed in fancy clothes.

Life long ago

Early Indians created beautiful vases and other works of art.

People lived in India thousands of years ago. The **ancient** Indians, or the Indians of long ago, were a **civilization**. A civilization is a group of people who share languages, government, arts, religion, and who are able to **record** their history. The ancient Indians studied math and science. They grew crops such as peas, sesame seeds, dates, and cotton. They also traded goods with other people who lived nearby.

Early Indian traders used elephants to carry goods from place to place.

Ancient Indians built towns and cities.
The buildings were made using clay bricks.

Europeans in India

Indian textiles, or cloths, are bright and colorful.

In 1498, people from Europe began trading goods with India. Traders from France, Portugal, England, and other countries fought to control the trade in India. They wanted the spices, **textiles**, and other fancy items that were made by Indians. England's East India Company became the most successful trading company in India. It controlled most of India for many years.

Traders from many countries traveled to India. They wanted the fine goods that were made there. This ship is sailing into Mumbai. The building below was built to welcome people who came to India by ship. It is called the Gateway.

Living under British rule

In 1858, India became an English **colony**. A colony is a place that is ruled by a faraway country. People from England came to live in India. These **colonists** took away the farms, animals, and other belongings of the Indians. The colonists also shipped India's **raw materials**, such as cotton, to factories in England to make goods from them. They then sold the goods back to the people of India. England became wealthy, whereas the people of India lived in **poverty**.

Being a British colony hurt the people of India. Many Indians still live in poverty.

Peaceful protests

The people of India did not want to be ruled by England. They wanted **independence**. Independence is the freedom to rule one's own country. In 1916, a man named Mohandas Gandhi began teaching Indians how to fight for their freedom. He asked them to stop buying British goods and showed them how to start their own businesses. He organized peaceful **protests** and marches.

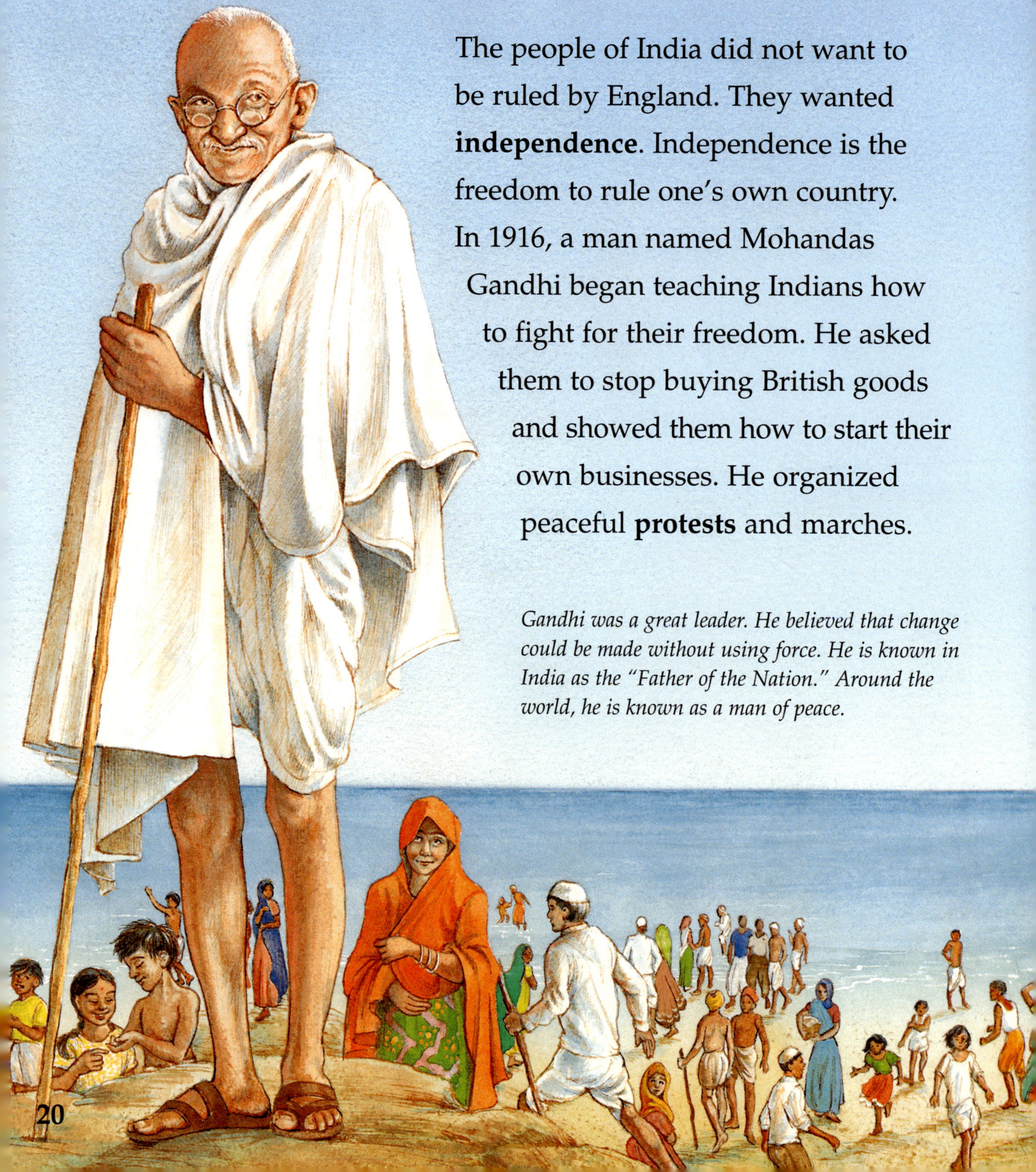

Gandhi was a great leader. He believed that change could be made without using force. He is known in India as the "Father of the Nation." Around the world, he is known as a man of peace.

India's independence

After many years, Gandhi's peaceful ways were successful. On August 15, 1947, India gained independence from England. A man named Jawaharlal Nehru became the first **prime minister** of India. A prime minister is the leader of a country.

Nehru worked hard to make the lives of children better. He built many schools across the country. These young Indians are going to school. They are getting a ride on a small ricksha.

India's government

Prime Minister Nehru helped create the new Indian **government**. A government is a group of people who are in charge of a country. The government makes important decisions and laws that the citizens of a country must follow. In 1950, the **Republic** of India was formed.

India's main government is in New Delhi. The Secretariat, shown here, is an important government building.

What is a democracy?

India's government is a **democracy**. In a democracy, the citizens of a country **elect**, or choose, their leaders. They elect them by voting. The prime minister is the head of the Indian government. The prime minister and the other members of the government run the country.

India's flag is painted on this child's face!

Saffron is a yellow-orange color.

The flag of India

India's flag is made up of three stripes. The **saffron** stripe stands for purity. The white stripe stands for peace and truth. The green stripe stands for India's rich soil and the plants that grow in it. The wheel in the middle of the flag stands for peaceful change and **justice**. Justice is fairness.

Holidays in India

There are many holidays in India. Some are **national holidays**. National holidays honor India's history. Republic Day is a national holiday. On January 26, Indians celebrate the day that India became a republic. On this day each year, there are colorful parades throughout the country.

The largest Republic Day parade is held in New Delhi. People from all over India come to watch.

Holi is a fun-filled spring festival. During Holi, people sing, dance, and put on plays. They splash one another with powders of spring colors.

To celebrate Diwali, people light oil lamps and float them down rivers. They also watch fireworks, eat sweets, and give gifts.

Weddings are huge celebrations in India. They last up to a week. Before a wedding, a bride's hands and feet are painted with ***mehndi****. Mehndi is like a tattoo done with a reddish brown dye called* ***henna****. The bride also wears a lot of jewelry. Grooms often arrive at weddings on horseback.*

Indian culture

Indian **culture** is a blend of old and new ways. Culture includes art, music, sports, food, and clothing. Indians perform songs, dances, and plays that are thousands of years old. They also enjoy watching movies and listening to modern music.

This woman is performing a traditional Indian dance.

*Street performers play music in India's city streets and bazaars. This father and son are playing folk fiddles called **ravanhasta**. They made the instruments themselves.*

Cricket is the most popular sport in India. People play it in fields across the country. Cricket is a lot like baseball, but it has different rules.

These people are in a ***yoga*** *class in India. Yoga is a set of gentle exercises. It was practiced in India thousands of years ago. Today, yoga is popular all over the world.*

Hooray for Bollywood!

Indians love going to the movies! Each week, millions of Indians line up to watch their favorite stars perform on the big screen. Many Indian movies are made in Mumbai. The nickname for that city's movie-making business is "Bollywood." Bollywood is a combination of the names Bombay and Hollywood. Bombay is Mumbai's old name.

Indian movies are popular in many countries, especially where a lot of Indian people live.

Indian food

India is known for its tasty and spicy food. Many Indian dishes are made with rice or wheat. These are **staple** foods in India. The dishes are flavored with **curry**, hot chili peppers, and other spices. Some of the flavors of India are shown on this page.

This picture shows some delicious dishes. Which one would you like to try?

These spices are for sale at an Indian bazaar.

naan

*Many Indians are **vegetarians**. Vegetarians do not eat meat. This woman is selling fresh vegetables at a market.*

*This woman is making **naan**. Naan is a puffy, oval-shaped bread.*

This Indian dish is flavored with curry and served with rice.

Indian clothing

Indian clothing is comfortable. It is made of cotton. Cotton helps keep people cool in hot weather. Both men's and women's clothing is colorful. Indian men wear loose trousers, skirts, or **dhotis**. A dhoti is cotton cloth that is wrapped around the waist and pulled between the legs. Many men also wear **turbans**, or long scarves wrapped around the head. Children wear both traditional and modern clothing.

*These people are wearing different kinds of clothes. The women are wearing **salwar-kameez** suits. Salwar are loose pants, and kameez are long dresses. Women also wear **shawls**, or wide scarves. Many young people wear modern clothing, such as jeans and T-shirts.*

*Many women wear **saris**. A sari is a long piece of cloth that is wrapped around a woman's body.*

Your own tour

There are many wonderful things to see in India. India has beautiful landscapes, amazing buildings, and great works of art. It is a very colorful country! If you visited India, which of these things would you like to do or see? This young woman will be your first guide. She lives in the Himalayas. The Himalayas are huge mountains. The tallest mountain on Earth, Mount Everest, is part of the Himalayas. These mountains form the border between India and China.

You could join this group of hikers. How far up the mountain could you climb?

At the end of your hike in the Himalayas, you would see the most beautiful sunset, with colors of pure gold.

*You might want to visit the Taj Mahal, the most popular place to see in India. This amazing building is a **tomb**. A tomb is a place where people are buried after they die. An Indian ruler built the Taj Mahal after his wife died. The Taj Mahal is a work of art. The sky behind it is also a work of art!*

*You could watch an exciting **kathakali** dance. Kathakali is music, painting, acting, story, and dance. The dancers wear great costumes!*

*You can find kathakali dancers in Kerala, a place in India. In Kerala, you can also go for boat rides in the **canals**. Will you go on a boat ride?*

Glossary

Note: Some boldfaced words are defined where they appear in the book.

canal A narrow, human-made waterway through which boats travel

capital The city in which a country's main government is located

coast The part of land that is near an ocean

colonist A person who lives in a colony

curry A spice that is made up of several kinds of spices; a dish flavored with curry

drought A long period without rain

earthquake A violent shaking of the ground caused by movement deep inside Earth

festival A special event or celebration

flood A large amount of water on land

official language The language used in government and business and which children are taught in school

poverty The state of having little money

protest A public act of disagreement

raw material A substance found in nature that can be used to make a product

record To set down, in writing or in drawings, events that happened at certain times in history

religion A set of beliefs about God or gods

republic A type of government that does not have kings or queens as leaders and whose leaders are elected by the people

staple A main product that is grown or made and is eaten or used every day

temple A building used for worship

textile Cloth that is made by weaving

traditional Describing ways that have been practiced for many years

well A deep hole in the ground from which people get water

vendor A person who sells something

Index